JOE BENNETT

Guitar Chords

...To Go!

WISE PUBLICATIONS
London / New York / Paris / Sydney / Copenhagen / Madrid

Exclusive Distributors:

MUSIC SALES LIMITED
14/15 Berners Street, London W1T 3LJ,
England.

MUSIC SALES PTY LIMITED
20 Resolution Drive, Caringbah, NSW 2229,
Australia.

MUSIC SALES CORPORATION
257 Park Avenue South, New York, NY10010
United States of America.

Order No. AM954240
ISBN 0-7119-7231-1
This book © Copyright 1998 by Wise Publications.

Written by Joe Bennett.
Book design and layout by Digital Music Art.
Cover design by Michael Bell Design.
Cover and text photographs by George Taylor.
Artist photographs courtesy of LFI.
Printed in the United Kingdom by
Caligraving Limited, Thetford, Norfolk.

Your Guarantee of Quality:
As publishers, we strive to produce
every book to the highest commercial standards.
The music has been freshly engraved and
the book has been carefully designed to
minimise awkward page turns and to
make playing from it a real pleasure.
Particular care has been given to specifying
acid-free, neutral-sized paper made from pulps
which have not been elemental chlorine bleached.
This pulp is from farmed sustainable
forests and was produced with special
regard for the environment.
Throughout, the printing and binding have
been planned to ensure a sturdy, attractive
publication which should give years of enjoyment.
If your copy fails to meet our high standards,
please inform us and we will gladly replace it.

Guitar Chords To Go!

How often have you looked in a chord book and seen a load of shapes you don't understand? Or even worse, played the chord line from a songbook only to find that the guitar part sounds nothing like the original recording?

Guitarists can learn in two different ways – study or trial and error. The only trouble is, sometimes the chords you study aren't the same as the ones you actually use when you're playing. The purpose of this book is to guide you through the chord shapes which guitarists use most of the time. It's not intended to cover every chord that was ever invented – there's no chapter on jazz, for example – but it does contain the shapes that the majority of working guitarists use when they're playing live or recording. We've even included 'lazy' shapes which, technically speaking, constitute 'bad' technique. But if everyone else is using these chords and creating great music with them, why should you miss out?

Diagrams Explained

Fretboxes

Fretboxes show the guitar upright *i.e.* with the headstock, nut and tuning pegs at the top of the picture – six vertical lines represent the strings.

The x symbol means you should not play this string

The o symbol means play the string 'open' without fretting a note

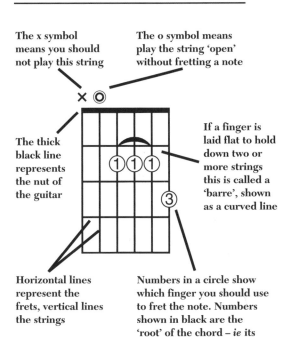

The thick black line represents the nut of the guitar

If a finger is laid flat to hold down two or more strings this is called a 'barre', shown as a curved line

Horizontal lines represent the frets, vertical lines the strings

Numbers in a circle show which finger you should use to fret the note. Numbers shown in black are the 'root' of the chord – *ie* its letter name

Notation and tablature

'Tab' is drawn with the guitar on its side, with the thickest string at the bottom – six horizontal lines represent the strings.

The top stave shows the chord as it would appear in traditional music notation

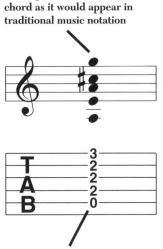

Below is the tablature – the numbers represent the fret positions. A zero means the string should be played open

Open Major Chords

One of the simplest and most common types of chord is the 'major'. They have a very simple, uncomplicated sound, and as such are often used in folk and country music. The major chords in this section are played in an 'open' position, meaning that one or more of the strings you strum is not fretted. Open chords are, most of the time, the easiest type to play.

You can hear major chords in almost every type of music. These examples have all been used at one time or another by artists as diverse as Buddy Holly, The Beatles, Bob Dylan, Oasis, The Eagles, Queen and The Verve. In gig set lists and chord sheets, they're generally referred to by their letter name only, so the word 'major' is omitted – *e.g.* C major is usually just referred to as C.

A

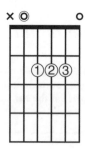  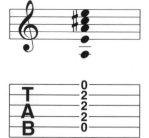

Don't strum the sixth (thickest) string. You may find it tricky to squeeze three fingers together in a row like this – some rock players cover all three notes by squeezing the second and third fingers together.

C

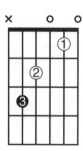  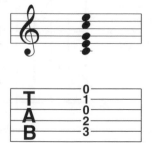

C is more difficult because one of the open strings comes between the fretted notes.

Keep all your fingers at right angles to the fingerboard to let the open strings ring freely.

C (version 2)

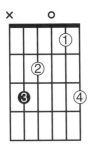  

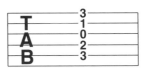

This version of the open C chord has a slightly fuller sound due to the top G note which is added by the little finger. It's often used by folk-rock acoustic players like Bob Dylan and Paul Simon.

D

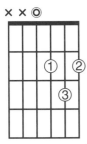  

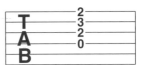

Most players think of D as a triangle shape on the neck. Avoid strumming the sixth and fifth strings.

E

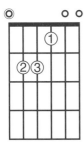  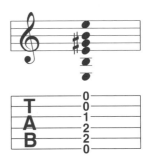

The chord beloved of Marc Bolan, John Lennon and Noel Gallagher. E has a rich, full sound, because it contains three open notes, and you can strum all six strings.

F

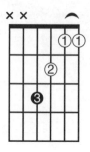  

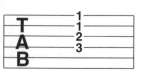

Although not strictly an open chord (*i.e.* it doesn't contain open strings) this easy F is shown here because of its 1st fret position. Note that the first finger is flattened across two strings in a 'barre'.

G

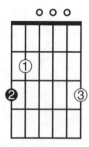  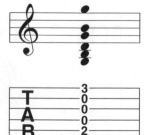

G is another full-sounding chord, but it can take work to master that nasty stretch between the second and third fingers. Make sure that you're not accidentally muting any of the open strings.

G (version 2)

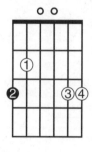  

Some guitarists play a G chord with four fingers, as shown here. It gives more of a rock feel, and you'll see it under the fingers of Tom Petty and Bruce Springsteen, among others.

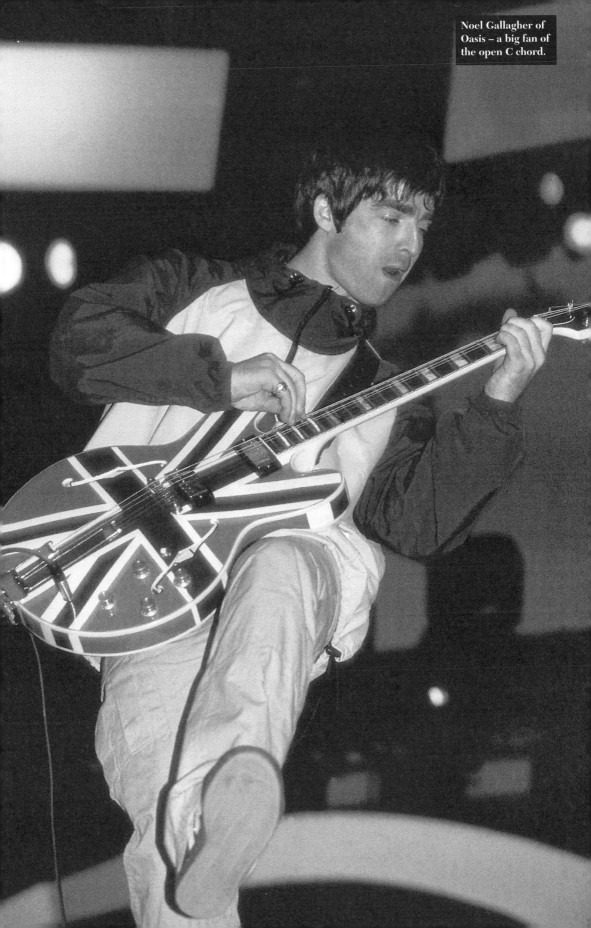

Noel Gallagher of Oasis – a big fan of the open C chord.

Open Minor Chords

I f every songwriter only ever played major chords, the world would never have heard Paul Weller's *Wild Wood*, John Lennon's *Working Class Hero* or Metallica's *Nothing Else Matters*. Minor chords have a melancholy edge which some musicians describe as 'sad-sounding', although this isn't always the case – check out the up-tempo verse of *I Wanna Be Like You* from the movie *The Jungle Book*, or the intro from the blues classic *Hit The Road Jack*.

The three minor chords shown here have been used in thousands of songs, and are among the first chords every guitar player needs to learn. Usually, they are combined with other types of chords (such as majors, 7ths, minor 7ths etc) – it's rare for a piece of music to feature minor chords alone.

Am

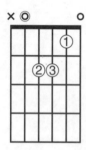  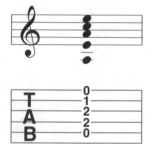

This is the first chord in The Animals' *House Of The Rising Sun* and The Rolling Stones' *Angie*, among many others. Make sure you don't catch the sixth string accidentally – this will make it sound muddy.

Dm

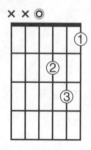   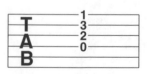

Although D minor is only a four-string chord (so don't strum the two bass strings) it has a slightly sweeter sound than A minor. Practise it until all four strings sound clearly.

Em

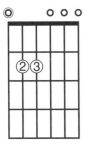

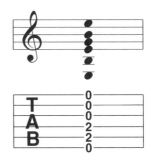

This dramatic-sounding chord is the easiest of the three minor shapes. As long as you make sure that both fingers are cleanly and accurately fretting the notes, E minor will always sound great.

John Lennon used open Am as the first chord of his song *Working Class Hero.*

eventh chords sound more complicated and colourful than their major and minor cousins. They come in three basic types – 'ordinary' 7ths (sometimes called dominant 7ths), major 7ths, and minor 7ths. You may notice that some of the major 7ths shapes are similar to their corresponding major chord, and some of the minor 7ths are similar to their corresponding minor chord.

For this reason, 7th-type chords are often used in place of more straightforward majors and minors.

Ordinary 7ths sometimes appear in blues, rock and R&B. Major 7ths have a wistful quality and consequently sound good in ballads. Minor 7ths can add a jazzy or funky sound to your chord sequence. Note the way they are abbreviated – 7, maj7 and m7.

A7

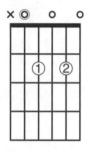  

This is basically an ordinary A chord with one finger taken off, though feel free to use different fingers from the ones shown here if you find it easier to make the notes sound clearly.

A7 (version 2)

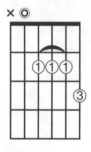  

Although it's less common than the basic shape, many players still prefer this version of A7. It's tricky though, because you have to barre across three strings with the first finger.

B7

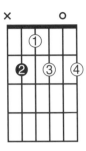   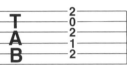

Yes, it's awkward, but the chord of B7 is essential to learn, not least because it appears in the most common guitar-based chord sequence in the world – the 12-bar blues in E.

C7

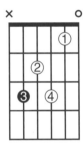   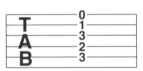

If you add your little finger to a normal C major chord you get this open version of C7. Hint – move this shape up two frets and play only the middle four strings for a different D7 (see page 38).

D7

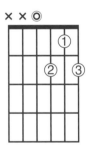  

This is the more common version of D7 though, as used by folkies the world over. It sounds very 'country' if you play it before or after a G chord, or more bluesy when it occurs after an A7 chord.

E7

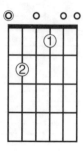  

If you're ever going to play the blues, you need this chord. It's another example of a major chord (E major) with a finger removed, creating a 7th. Make sure the open fourth string rings clearly.

F#7

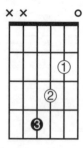  

Although you don't see this chord as often as some of the others in this chapter, it's a useful open chord in its own right – note that it's quite similar to the F shape on page 6.

G7

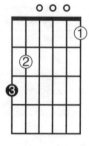  

The open chord of G7 looks similar to an ordinary G major (page 6), but check out that fingering – you'll find that you have to move all three fingers to change between the chords of G and G7.

Am7

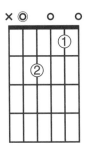  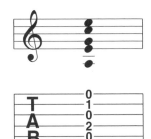

Take a finger off an A minor chord and you get
open Am7. Note that the sixth string is not played.

Dm7

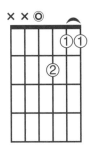  

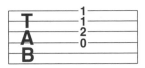

This chord can be played with the first finger
flattened over two strings, as shown here, or by
using three separate fingers for the three fretted
notes. This is the version most people find easiest.

Em7

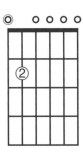  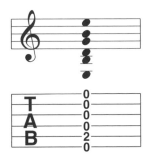

One finger and five open strings – what could be
simpler than that?!

Paul Simon used the dreamy sound of major 7th chords in the songs of Simon & Garfunkel.

Amaj7

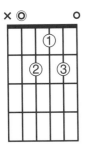  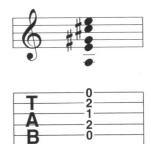

Although the fingering of this chord appears to be similar to the open D7 (page 11), it sounds very different. Try playing a chord of A, followed by Amaj7, followed by A7 for a classic Beatles effect.

Cmaj7

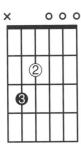   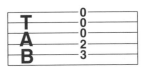

Play a C chord, then remove the first finger, letting the open second string sound as shown.

Dmaj7

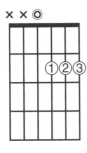   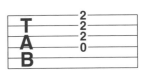

Dmaj7 can be played either of two ways – with three separate fingers, as shown here, or with one finger flattened across the first three strings. Make sure the open fourth string rings clearly.

Emaj7

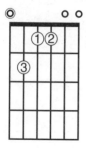  

This open maj7 shape is not used by many players because it sometimes jars slightly on the ear, but there are times (especially in country strumming or single-note picked chord parts) when it works fine.

Fmaj7

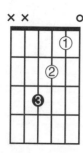   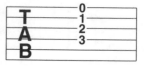

This 'diagonal' shape sounds lovely when it's played before or after a C or Cmaj7 chord.

Gmaj7

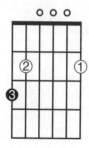  

This is the big, expansive chord that is played in the verse of The Eagles' track *Lyin' Eyes*.

Glenn Frey of The Eagles – major seventh man.

4

Barre Chords

Barre chords are so-called because one of the fretting hand's fingers is pressed against two or more strings (this is shown as a curved line in the fretbox). They can be moved up or down the neck to different fret positions to create new chords. The advantage of this is that once you've learned one new barre shape, you've in effect learned 12 new chords!

Below are diagrams showing the names of the notes on the sixth and fifth strings. To find any barre chord, look at the fretbox to see whether the root note (shown in a black circle) appears on the fifth or sixth string, then move the barre shape up or down until you reach the desired pitch. For example, a chord of A♭ (also known as G♯) can be played using an 'F shape' moved up to the 4th fret.

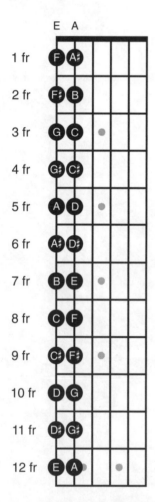

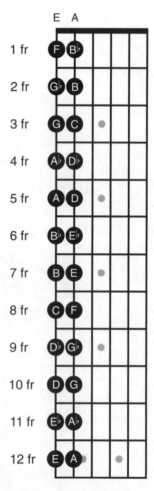

This diagram shows how to find any barre chord position, and will help you if the chord you want has a sharp (♯) in its name. All of the F-based barre shapes in this book (see opposite) have their root on the sixth string – the Bb-based ones have theirs on the fifth.

Use this version if the chord you want has a flat (♭) in its name. Both of these diagrams can be used to find any barre chord which has its root on the sixth or fifth string – simply select the type you want (minor, maj7, 7 etc) then find the letter name (F, G, D♭ etc) on the fingerboard.

F

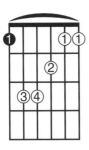  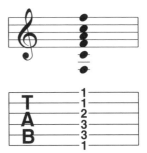

The F barre shape has its root on the sixth string. Move it up one fret and you get F♯, up two and you get G. You can even play it way up at the 12th fret to create a barre chord of E.

B♭

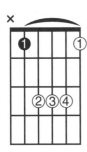 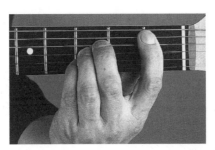  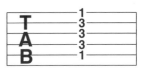

Any B♭-based barre shape has its root on the fifth string. Sometimes, if you're changing chords quickly, it's easier to change between the F and B♭ shapes because it involves less hand movement.

B♭ *'lazy version'*

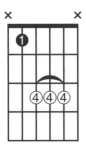   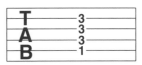

Lots of rock players favour this version of B♭– it sounds nearly as full, and is far easier to play.

Do make sure that you don't flatten the finger all the way over – the first string should not sound.

John Squire's guitar work with the Stone Roses in the 1980s featured lots of big, full-sounding barre chords.

Fm

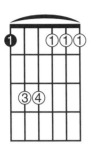  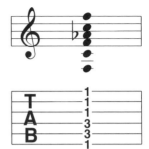

For this, the same principle applies as for the F major shape – move it up one fret and you get F#m, move it up one more and you get Gm, and so on all the way up to Em at the 12th fret.

B♭m

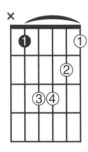   

This minor shape has its root on the 5th string, so could create a chord of Bm if played at the 2nd fret, Cm at the 3rd etc. Its sweet tone makes it especially good for funk, jazz and dance music.

F7

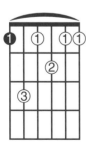  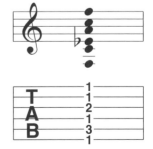

Although this barre version of F7 looks very similar to the ordinary barre F shape, it's quite difficult to make that barred fourth string sound clearly in the middle of the chord.

F7 (version 2)

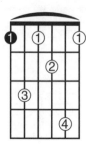

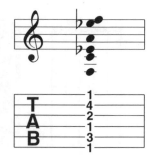

Add your little finger to the chord and you get this more colourful-sounding version of F7. It's a tricky stretch though, so ensure that all of the notes sound clearly as you strum across it.

B♭7

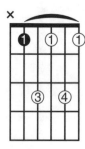

This is a barre version of the ordinary open A7 shape (see page 10). Note that the root is on the fifth string. This means that there's a chord of B7 at the 2nd fret, C7 at the 3rd, and A7 up at the 12th.

Fmaj7

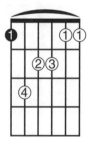

Many players like to omit the first string when they play this chord because it clashes a bit with the note on the fourth string. Like all the other chords in this section, it can be moved to any fret.

B♭maj7

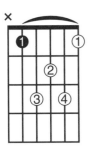  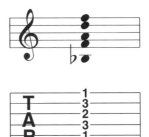

This version of the major seventh barre chord is more common, and sounds 'sweeter' than the F shape opposite. Note that the barre doesn't have to press all the strings – just the fifth and first.

Fm7

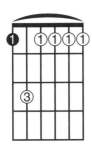  

Another six-string chord, this time with a barre covering all but one of the strings. Some funk players choose a 'partial chord' version, just using the first finger flattened over the first three strings.

B♭m7

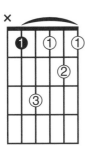  

This difficult but versatile chord shape sounds just as good at the 13th fret as it does at the 1st. Try sliding into it as you strum rhythmic patterns for a funky 1970s disco sound.

5

Power Chords

Power chords (also called '5' chords) are the sound behind almost every rock and metal band ever, from Black Sabbath to Metallica. They have a strident, aggressive feel, and sound good with lots of distortion (try comparing an F5 power chord and an F major with the overdrive levels cranked right up – the F5 wins every time). As with the barre chords in the previous section, the F and B♭ versions of the chords can be moved up to any fret using the fingerboard diagrams on page 18. However, there are some great examples which feature open strings, and I've included these too. Power chords are also useful for making up your own rock riffs – try moving the chord around the neck while you play downstrokes on the bass strings with the plectrum.

F5

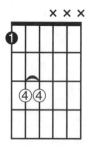  

With this moveable power chord there are two choices – either play the three bass strings as shown, or only hit the sixth and fifth strings. Remember to mute the other three strings.

B♭5

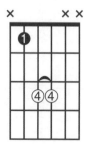   

Sometimes you may not need to move the F5 shape all over the neck – there may be a version of the power chord you want with its root on the fifth string.

A5

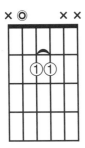

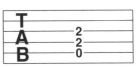

This open power chord appears at the beginning of *Won't Get Fooled Again* by The Who, *Tie Your Mother Down* by Queen, plus many a pub blues standard. It's a stripped-down version of A major.

A5 (version 2)

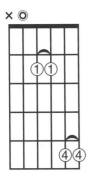

This version of A5 covers three octaves, so it has an even more powerful sound. If you have trouble flattening the little finger over two strings, do persevere – the effort will be worth it!

C5

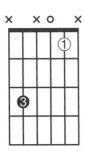
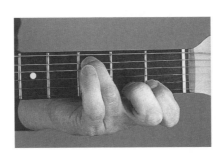

Although this is not a commonly-used shape, it's interesting because it uses muting techniques to stop some strings from sounding. Famously used in ZZ Top's *Gimme All Your Lovin'*.

The razorless ZZ Top – their single Gimme All Your Lovin' relied on the sound of a C5 chord.

D5

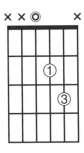   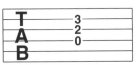

Like the open A5 on page 25, this is just a simplified version of the equivalent major chord.

You might find, though, that a fretted version (B 5 shape at the 5th fret) sounds more convincing.

D5 (version 2)

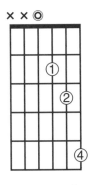   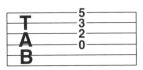

Here's a more spaced-out version of the same chord. Try adding distortion and delay, then picking across the strings one-by-one for a typical rock-anthem-type guitar intro.

E5

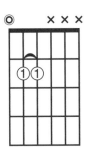  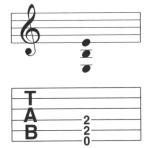

This is the lowest, thickest-sounding power chord anywhere on the guitar fingerboard. It sounds great played with downstrokes as a rock or blues accompaniment part.

E5 (version 2)

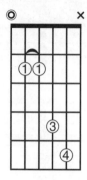  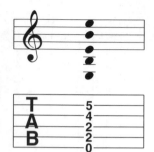

This is an expanded version of the more common three-string version (previous page). The first and second strings can, if so desired, be played open for a more 'jangly' sound.

F5 (version 2)

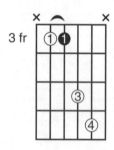  

Although this version of F5 is moveable, its root is actually on the fourth string. So it creates G5 when played at the 5th fret, A♭5 at the 6th, and D5 way up at the 12th.

G5

 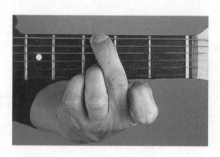 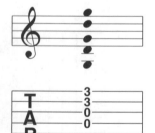

If you omit the 5th string from the easy G major chord shown on page 6, you get this powerful alternative to a G5 barre shape. Use the side of the second finger to mute the 5th string.

Tony Iommi of Black Sabbath wrote dozens of rock riffs by simply moving power chord shapes around the neck.

6

Suspended Chords

Suspended chords are so-called because one of the notes has been taken out and replaced with a different note which isn't part of a major or minor chord – so a note is 'suspended'. What's more, they have an unfinished, suspended-in-space sound to them too. Sus chords, as they're known, comes in two types – sus2 and sus4, of which sus4 is the most common. They are rarely used on their own, because of their incomplete sound they nearly always 'resolve' to a more straightforward chord such as a major or minor. Check out the intro to Crowded House's *Don't Dream It's Over*, the strummed chords at the end of the chorus from The Beatles' *You've Got To Hide Your Love Away*, or The Who's *Pinball Wizard* (shown on page 44).

Fsus4

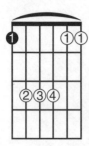  

This is the standard six-string sus4 with its root on the sixth string. As with all F type barre chords, it can be moved to any fret position using the fingerboard diagrams on page 18.

B♭sus4

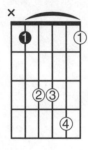  

The other moveable sus4 shape has its root on the fifth string. Slide the little finger back one fret and you've got an ordinary B♭ barre shape, making the change from sus4 to major chord really easy.

B♭sus2

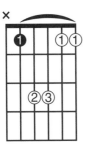  

If you play this moveable sus2 barre shape at the 6th fret, that's the intro chord from *Don't Dream* *It's Over* by Crowded House. Resolve this shape to a major chord by simply adding the little finger.

Asus2

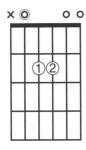  

Much beloved of acoustic-playing songwriters, Asus2 sounds more complicated and difficult than it really is. Try making up riffs using combinations of A, Asus4 (see below) and Asus2.

Asus4

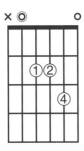  

If you're playing a song that starts on a chord of D, wait until you get to a chord of A in the music, and try playing Asus4, followed by A. This is called a 'resolution' and is a useful songwriting tool.

Bsus4

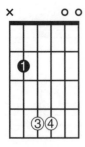

The note of B (at the 4th fret, third string) is doubled by the open second string, creating a 12-string guitar effect. This shape appears in Suzanne Vega's song *Luka*.

Csus4

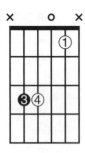

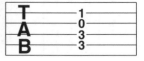

As long as you only play the middle four strings, this is a much easier alternative than the barre shape Csus4 at the 3rd fret. If you use this fingering, it's easy to resolve to a normal C chord.

Dsus2

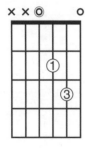

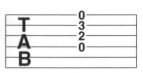

Play a D chord and take one finger off to create the chord of Dsus2. John Lennon used a combination of sus2, major, and sus4 chords like this to write *Happy Xmas (War Is Over)*.

Dsus4

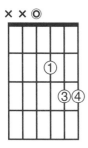

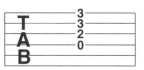

Many players like to keep their second finger at the 2nd fret on the first string (i.e. just one fret behind the little finger), in readiness for changing the Dsus4 back to a D.

Esus4

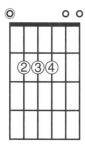
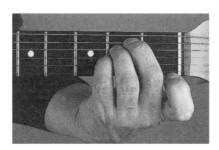
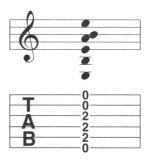

A similar idea can apply to Esus4, which resolves easily to a straight chord of E. Bear in mind, though, that including the open third string actually creates a chord of Em, not Esus2.

Gsus4

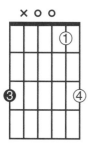

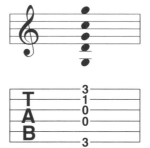

This less-used open sus4 chord is most useful if you're playing it on an acoustic, because it uses two open strings in the middle of the chord. Playing the first string is optional.

Other Useful Open Chords

Sometimes, a particular shape or fingering might create a chord with a complex-sounding name, even if it's really easy to play. Shown here are some of the common examples you may see in songbooks. These shapes are particularly good for acoustic songwriting because they sound colourful and complex, helping to suggest melodies and ideas. All of these examples contain at least one open string, and none of them use barres.

You may notice that most of these examples are simply familiar chords with one or more of the notes replaced by an open string. You can apply this idea to almost any chord you know: experiment and see what happens.

Tip – if it doesn't sound good, try moving the whole shape to a different fret position.

A add9

  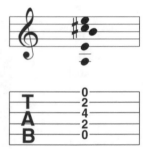

This chord is an adaption of the open A chord shape (see page 4), but take note of the finger number changes that are necessary to accommodate the stretch. It has a laid-back, 'Joni Mitchell' sound.

C add9

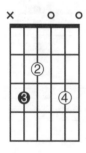  

Much beloved of Noel Gallagher, this is a C chord with the little finger added at the 3rd fret. It works especially well with songs which start or end on a G chord. The open first string can be omitted.

Em^{add9}

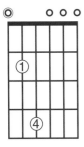  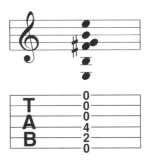

Although this chord isn't that great if you just strum it up and down, try picking across the notes one at a time – that clash in the middle of the chord sounds kind of 'heavy metal intro', doesn't it?

Fmaj7^{#11}

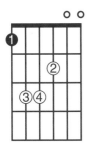  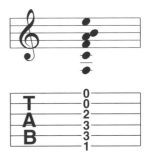

Don't be put off by the jazzy-sounding name here – this is a great chord. Again, it's most effective when you pick the notes one at a time, but it can work with fingerstyle picking techniques too.

G6

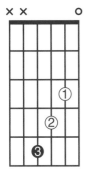 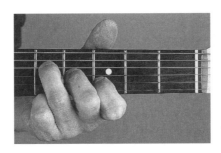 

If you move the Fmaj7 shown on page 16 up two frets, you get this version of G6, as used by Keith Richards in the Rolling Stones' *Angie*, and at the end of The Beatles' *She Loves You*.

8

Slashed Chords

Many chord books and song transcriptions feature 'slashed' chords, which confuses some guitarists because they don't know whether to play the chord on the left or the right of the slash. Here's how they work – the bit before the slash refers to the chord name itself; and the bit after is simply a single bass note. So A/G, for example, means a chord of A with a note of G in the bass. If you're playing in a band, it's normally OK for the guitarist to play the chord before the slash and the bass player to play the single bass note. If you're playing unaccompanied, you need to figure out a way to finger the chord *and* bass note; I've shown some examples here. Remember, any chord can have an alternative bassnote – try figuring out some of your own.

A/G

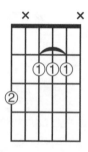 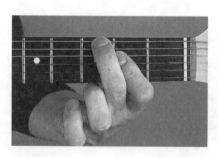 

Although it's possible to play a straight A chord in the normal way and reach across with the little finger for the bass note, this version, with the first finger flattened across three strings, is much easier.

D/F#

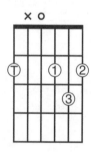  

Some guitar teachers will give you a slap on the wrist for hanging your thumb over the top of the neck like this, but Jimi Hendrix, Paul Simon and dozens of folk players can't all be wrong…

G/A

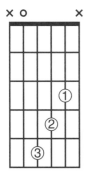

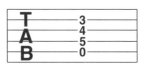

Of course, there's no reason why the bassnote shouldn't be an open string. The chord of G/A is sometimes referred to as A11, and it has a very warm, jazzy sound.

C/B

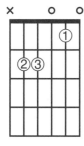
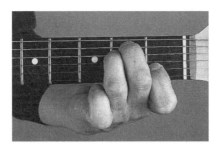

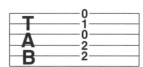

Here, the root note of an ordinary C chord has simply been dropped down a fret. Paul Simon uses it in the acoustic rhythm part from Simon & Garfunkel's hit *America*.

D/C

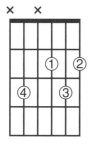

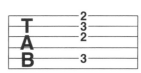

As with the A/G (opposite page), the side of the little finger is used to stop an open string from sounding. It's the second chord in the verse of The Beatles' *Dear Prudence*.

9

Alternative Chord Shapes

laying a rhythm part doesn't always mean using the shapes you'll find in a chord encyclopaedia. Lots of pro players use less conventional shapes, either because they work better in the context of a band mix; because they're more convenient to play at the time; or simply because they prefer the sound. Here, I've shown two moveable chords which chord books

sometimes miss out, plus three examples of 'partial chords'. Basically, a partial chord simply means missing out some of the notes of the chord – usually the lower ones in the bass range. Players as diverse as Nile Rogers of Chic, Prince, Steve Craddock of Ocean Colour Scene, or Eric Clapton have all used partial chords at one time or another. Any chord can be played as a partial shape.

D7   *'Middle D7'*

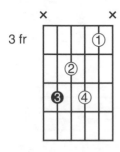
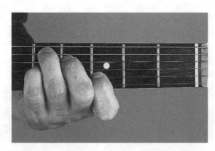

So-called because it doesn't use the outer two strings, this fretted shape is handy in many differ- ent styles, though it's perhaps most common in Rock 'n' Roll or Rhythm & Blues.

D   *'Folky C shape'*

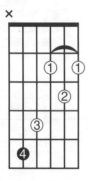

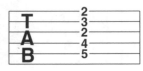

If you look carefully you'll notice that this is just a C chord moved up two frets, with a barre over the first three strings. Many players actually prefer this version to a conventional barre chord shape.

F (partial)

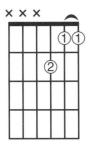 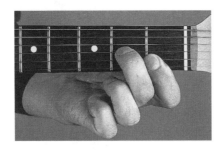  

The simplest way to create a partial chord is to look at any chord you already know – and don't play all of the notes. This is a chord of F with some of the lower notes removed.

Dm (partial)

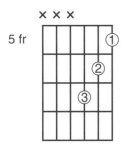 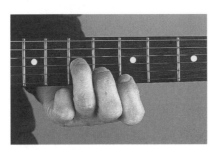  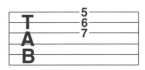

This chord is based on a Dm barre at the 5th fret, but because you're not playing any of the bass notes, you don't need the barre. Try playing this shape while someone else plays an ordinary Dm.

A7 (partial)

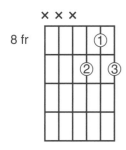   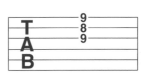

Although this isn't based on a conventional barre chord, it's still a valid seventh chord shape – it's basically an open D7 chord (as shown on page 11), moved up 7 frets.

Andy Summers
– moonwalking
chord shapes.

There is a small number of chords that have become classics in their own right because they're instantly recognisable. The fourteen examples shown here have all been associated with a particular song, and some have been the subject of much debate among guitarists as to how they should be played!

Each of them should be identifiable if you just strum across the whole chord once, with the exception of the Chuck Berry example, which will need repeated up and down strumming.

Don't be put off by the fact that many of these chords have complex-sounding theoretical names – people are far more likely to know a chord as 'the end bit of James Bond' than they are to care about it being called E minor (major 9th)!

G7sus4/A   *'A Hard Day's Night'*

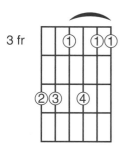

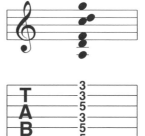

This may sound slightly different from the Beatles' record because it was originally played on an electric 12-string. Nevertheless, this is how George Harrison played it, back in 1964.

Dm7add11   *'Walkin' On The Moon'*

This Police song would not have been complete without the 'chang' of this great-sounding chord on Andy Summers' Fender Telecaster. Add a C barre chord and you can play along with the bass riff.

Em^{maj9} '007'

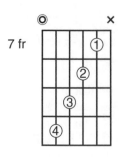

7 fr

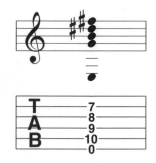

The James Bond Theme ends with this ominous-sounding chord, played in 1960 by session guitarist Vic Flick. Use the side of the fretting hand's first finger to mute the first string.

E7^{#9} 'The Hendrix chord'

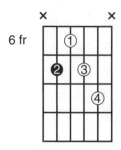

6 fr

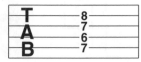

Foxy Lady, Purple Haze, Voodoo Chile... All three of these Jimi Hendrix classics have featured this chord. The open first and sixth strings are optional in each case, making the chord sound fuller.

D^{aug} 'No Particular Place To Go'

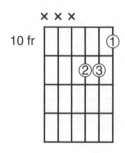

10 fr

This partial chord, played up and down rapidly a total of 13 times, forms the intro to Chuck Berry's famous rock 'n' roll tune. The rest of the song uses chords of G7, C7 and D7.

Cmaj7   *'Design For Life'*

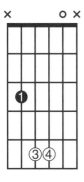

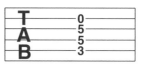

Pick across the strings one by one, starting on the root note, until you get to the second string, then pick back in the other direction. It's the first part of the Manic Street Preachers' *Design For Life*.

D & Dsus4   *'Crazy Little Thing Called Love'*

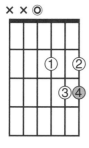

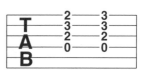

Play a normal D chord , then add and remove the little finger at the third fret (shown in grey) while you're strumming. That's the intro to this Queen single, from their 1980 album 'The Game'.

E/D   *'Hole Hearted'*

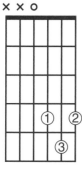

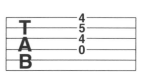

Play a D chord twice, then slide it up two frets and pick the strings one by one. Nuno Bettencourt plays this on an acoustic just before the verse section from Extreme's hit *Hole Hearted*.

E5   *'Paranoid'*

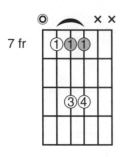  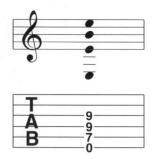

Because of the partial barre behind two of the fretted notes, you can play hammer-ons between the 7th and 9th fret, as Tony Iommi does in the intro from this early Black Sabbath recording.

E9   *'James Brown'*

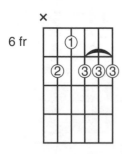   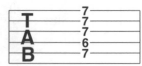

This funky ninth chord shape appears in a long list of James Brown tunes, and is one of the most commonly-used chords in '70s funk and disco. Try sliding up to the chord as you strum rapidly.

Bsus4 & B   *'Pinball Wizard'*

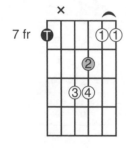  

You need to reach the thumb over the top of the neck to reach the bass note here. Use fast up and down strums while you add and remove the little finger note at the 9th fret.

C#5add9   *'Message In A Bottle'*

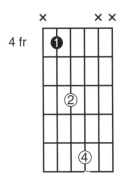

Here's another chord from a Police track. Most of the time, when 5add9 type chords appear in a song, they're picked one note at a time rather than strummed right across.

A & D/A   *'All Right Now'*

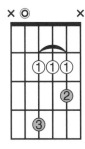

The D/A shape is played after a straight A chord in one of Paul Kossoff's guitar parts from this track by '70s rock-blues band Free. It also appears in Queen's *Hammer To Fall*.

Fsus2   *'Live Forever'*

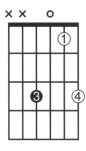

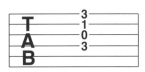

At the end of the chorus from this early Oasis hit, Noel Gallagher cranks up the distortion levels as he picks out a riff using the notes from this open chord shape.

I n my experience as a guitar examiner and teacher, it has always amazed me that so many candidates find rhythm playing their weakest area. When you consider that your average working guitarist spends around 95% of the time playing chord accompaniment, it seems odd that some players only ever want to learn riffs or solos.

There are many styles of music – Rock 'n' Roll, Rhythm & Blues, Reggae, Indie-rock, Britpop, even some rock and jazz – where the guitarist hardly ever plays a lead part.

Listed below are some bits of advice to help you maintain and improve the standard of your chord playing. I've also explained some of the common naming conventions that musicians may use when writing out chord sheets or 'charts' for guitar players.

Rhythm Tips

- Sometimes just two or three notes will sound better than a full chord.

- Arpeggio techniques – *i.e.* picking out the notes of a chord one by one in time with the music – can make a rhythm guitar part more interesting.

- In rock music, especially if you're using distortion, power chords usually work better than other types.

- When you're using barre chords, don't just move an F shape up and down the neck. You may find there's a B♭ shape which is easier to get to.

- If a string is marked with an X in the fret-box, it's very important that you don't play it, because it will interfere with the sound of the chord.

- If you get fret buzz in a chord, move the fingers closer to the next fret – that way you'll need less pressure to get the strings sounding clearly.

- When learning a piece of music from a chart, don't stop and pause every time there's a difficult chord change. Attempt the whole piece at a slower tempo so you keep the changes in time. The speed will come with practice.

- Play with other musicians and singers whenever you can – it's the best and quickest way to improve your timing, technique and chord knowledge.

Naming Conventions

Because of the different styles of guitarists throughout the world, several notation 'standards' have evolved. Below are several examples, all shown with a root note of C. On the left is printed the way you'll see chords in this book (usually the most common), followed by alternative namings.

C	C major, Cmaj
Cm	Cmin, C-
C7	Cdom7
Cmaj7	CM7, C△, C△7
Cm7	Cmin7, C-7
C5	$C^{(no\ 3rd)}$
Caug	C+, C^{+5}
C7#9	$C7^{(-10)}$, $C7^{(\flat10)}$

Finally, if you don't know a chord, there's usually one that you do know which will fit just as well. Here are a few tips;

- Chords ending in 9, 11 or 13 can usually be replaced with an equivalent 7th – *eg* if you don't know Cm11, Cm7 should be OK. If you can't play C9, try C7, and so on.

- In most cases, straight major or minor chords will work instead of 7ths or 9ths.

- Power chords (eg C5, A5 etc) can be used as a substitute for any major or minor chord, including 7ths, 9ths etc.